# WHAT HAPPENS TO YOUR BODY
# WHEN YOU ARE WEIGHT TRAINING

I CORONA BREZINA I

rosen publishing's
**rosen central**

New York

Published in 2010 by The Rosen Publishing Group, Inc.
29 East 21st Street, New York, NY 10010

Copyright © 2010 by The Rosen Publishing Group, Inc.

First Edition

**Library of Congress Cataloging-in-Publication Data**

Brezina, Corona.
What happens to your body when you are weight training / Corona Brezina.—
1st ed.
    p. cm.—(The how and why of exercise)
Includes bibliographical references and index.
ISBN-13: 978-1-4358-5307-2 (library binding)
1. Weight training—Juvenile literature. 2. Physical fitness—Juvenile literature.
3. Exercise—Juvenile literature. I. Title.
GV546.2.B74 2010
613.7'13—dc22

                                                                2008055611

*Manufactured in Malaysia*

# CONTENTS

# INTRODUCTION

Everybody knows that exercise is important. But many people don't know the extent to which getting into shape can improve their health and well-being. People who are physically fit are more likely to live a long life. They are less likely to suffer from numerous medical conditions ranging from stroke to cancer. There are also lifestyle benefits: People who exercise have more energy and a stronger immune system. They are also less likely to experience depression, stress, or disturbed sleep. For people who want to lose weight, a program that combines dieting and exercise is more likely to be effective than dieting alone.

A fitness plan should include three components: cardiovascular exercise (often called "cardio"), flexibility training, and weight training. Cardiovascular activities strengthen the heart and lungs. During such exercise, you breathe harder and your heart rate increases. Running, biking, swimming, and skiing are all activities that improve your cardiovascular health. Cardiovascular exercise also burns a lot of calories, which makes it an essential component of any weight-loss plan.

Flexibility training enables you to maintain ease of motion at the joints. As people grow older, the connective tissues at their joints shorten and tighten. Movements become stiff and difficult.

Weight training can improve health and quality of life regardless of age and fitness level. This is especially true when it is combined with a healthy diet and other forms of exercise.

This process can be prevented, to an extent, by flexibility training. Many people accomplish this through a stretching regimen. Practices like yoga and tai chi, two disciplines with Asian origins, can help maintain and improve flexibility as well.

Weight training builds strength and preserves the health of muscles, bones, and connective tissues. Weight training is not just for bodybuilders or exercise fanatics. It's great for people of any age or fitness level. An exercise program doesn't have to be intensive and time consuming. A half hour or so of physical activity daily can yield benefits. In addition to exercise, a nutritious diet is essential for lifelong health.

# Weight-Training Basics

## CHAPTER 1

Weight training is an essential component of any fitness program. It increases both physical strength and muscular endurance. In addition, weight training can improve bone strength, help control weight, boost stamina, and prevent injuries. It can also improve a person's confidence and self-image.

Although the phrase "weight training" might conjure up images of bodybuilders spending hours in the gym, weight training should not be considered a niche form of exercise. Anybody who wants to maintain lifelong physical health should pursue weight training. Nonetheless, it is a good idea to check with a doctor before beginning any exercise program, especially if you've been inactive or have certain medical conditions. A doctor can give advice on taking precautions when beginning the program.

Weight training is also known as strength training and resistance training. No matter what term is used, it describes the process that builds strength by adding resistance, which stresses the muscles. (In some cases, however, "resistance training" refers to a specific form of strength training.)

## Weight-Training Gear

Someone new to weight training may be amazed by the range of

A trainer at a gym helps a woman perform an exercise. In weight-training jargon, an "exercise" is a specific move intended to strengthen a particular muscle.

equipment. Different machines and exercises target different muscles in the body. A gym can provide a variety of machines, weights, and other forms of resistance equipment. But it's also possible to do some weight training at home with basic equipment.

Free weights are metal bars that have weights on either end. They are called "free weights" because unlike machines, they do not limit the body to a specific pattern of movement. There are two types of free weights: dumbbells and barbells. Dumbbells are short weights that range from 1 pound (0.45 kilograms) to more than 100 pounds (45 kg). They are generally used in pairs, one dumbbell for each hand. Barbells—often referred to as "bars"—range from 5 to 7 feet (1.5 to 2.1 meters) in length. They generally weigh between 25 and 45 pounds (11.3 and 20.4 kg). To increase the total weight,

Weight training improves both strength (the maximum amount of weight a person can lift) and muscular endurance (the ability to sustain lifting a weight over a period of time).

round plates are added to each end of the bar and secured with devices called collars. The plates weigh from 1.25 to 45 pounds (0.57 to 20.4 kg).

Many free-weight exercises require you to lie, sit, or kneel on a weight bench. This is a narrow padded bench that may be flat, vertical, or tilted. Some weight benches can be adjusted.

Weight machines may look scary, but they are actually a good starting point for beginners. For many machines, you only need to set the resistance, adjust the machine as necessary (such as by changing the seat height), and fasten the seat belt, if needed. Each machine isolates certain muscle groups. You complete the exercise at one machine and then move on to another.

There are a wide variety of specialized weight machines. Variable resistance machines—the best known is the Nautilus machine—adjust the resistance as the exercise is performed. As a result, resistance is constant throughout the exercise. The Smith machine consists of a barbell set within a track that restricts it to moving up and down. Many bar exercises can be done using the Smith machine, which increases stability and safety. Some of the newest weight machines have high-tech features that can remember your workout record and automatically set your preferences.

## Pros and Cons

There are advantages and disadvantages to both free weights and machines. Free weights are more versatile, since there are hundreds of free-weight exercises that strengthen every muscle in the body. Machines, by contrast, target a couple of specific muscles. Free weights allow more movement; machines restrict the range of motion. Free weights require that you balance and control the weights, which can strengthen stabilizer muscles—muscles other than the targeted muscles. Weight machines isolate muscle groups. Free weights require more skill, and some exercises should be performed with a spotter on hand, someone to help you if you can't lift the weights. A dropped weight or the improper handling of free weights can cause injury. Machines are safer and usually don't require spotters.

For free-weight lifters, there is the choice between dumbbells and barbells. The decision is largely a matter of personal preference, but there are advantages to each. Dumbbells allow you to work each side of the body independently, for example. This is useful when one side of the body—the dominant side—is stronger than the other. Bars offer more stability and the ability to lift heavier weights than when lifting dumbbells.

In order to avoid injury, use good form when lifting weights off the rack, carrying them, or returning them to the rack. Also, take care to avoid smashing your fingers!

A number of other weight-training options can add variety to your workouts. Ankle weights can make lower-body exercises more effective. Elastic tubes and bands are convenient and inexpensive weight-training tools. They come in varying lengths, shapes, and levels of resistance. The most basic weight exercises employ your own body weight. Push-ups, pull-ups, and crunches build strength with no equipment. Performing exercises in water is also a form of weight training, since water provides resistance to movement. Using gear like water dumbbells or gloves can further increase resistance.

Appropriate clothing and accessories make a workout safer and more comfortable. Clothes should allow free movement, but they should not be so loose that they could get caught in the machines. The best shoes are athletic shoes that provide support and traction. Weight lifters may wear gloves to protect their hands and prevent weights from slipping. Some people wear tight, wide weight belts; wrist wraps; or knee wraps during their workouts for extra support. Many experts, however, say that wearing belts and wraps can hinder muscle development, which could eventually lead to health consequences.

## Starting a Program

Knowing the equipment is only the first step in beginning weight training. Weight training has its own jargon, which is easy to pick up. Doing an exercise a single time—such as one push-up—is one repetition, or rep. Several reps performed without

# Training for Competition

The most serious weight lifters show off their abilities in competitions. In two types of competitive weight lifting, Olympic lifting and power lifting, athletes compete to see who can lift the most weight. Events in power lifting include the bench press and squat (both standard in gyms) and the dead lift (a more advanced lift). Olympic lifters perform two highly advanced lifts: the snatch and the "clean and jerk." In bodybuilding contests, competitors are judged on muscle size and appearance, not strength.

stopping is a set. The number of reps in one set varies depending on your fitness goals. A typical set consists of ten to twelve reps. Beginners should start out with one set of an exercise. Performing two or more sets can help build endurance. A routine—or workout or program—is your overall weight-training plan, which includes types of exercises, numbers of reps and sets, order of performance, and rest time. Your program will probably change as you reach some goals and set others.

Another important aspect of weight training is form, the proper technique for executing each exercise. Good form is essential in order to strengthen the targeted muscle. If you rock, lean forward, or arch your back for some exercises, you may cheat

A woman performs an exercise called a squat, which strengthens the legs. In general, you should keep weights close to the body and avoid twisting the body while lifting in order to prevent injury.

the muscle you are trying to strengthen by using other muscles to complete the exercise. In addition, good form is necessary for safety. For example, you should not bend your wrists too much when lifting or pulling weights in many exercises.

One of the key questions in weight training is the matter of how much weight to lift. There is no simple answer because appropriate weights vary depending on an individual's abilities, the size of the muscle, and which muscle or muscles are worked in the exercise. As a rule of thumb, the final rep in a set should be a challenge. It's better to start by erring on the side of caution in order to reduce any risk of injury. When a certain weight has become too easy to manage, you can try increasing it by 5 percent.

To increase your strength, you should train at least twice a week for a minimum of twenty minutes. Your workout should include exercises for every major muscle group. A muscle should rest for forty-eight hours after being exercised. Some athletes weight train using a split routine so that they can exercise on consecutive days without damaging any muscles. For example, they may devote two days to working their upper body and two days to the lower body.

# Weight Training and the Body

## CHAPTER 2

Anybody with a serious or even casual interest in weight training should spend some time learning about muscles and how they work. There are three types of muscles in the human body: cardiac, smooth, and skeletal. Cardiac muscle is the muscle tissue that makes up the heart. Smooth muscle tissue occurs in the walls of internal organs of the body. Skeletal muscles are the muscles that control movement and posture. These are the muscles that are targeted by weight training. Since they are attached to bones by tendons, muscles and bones are referred to as the musculoskeletal system.

When you move a muscle, it contracts and exerts a force on a tendon, which moves a bone. Muscles consist of bundles of cells called fibers. The contraction of a muscle is triggered by signals from the nervous system. Weight training increases strength by increasing the size of muscle fibers. It also works to improve the coordination of the nervous system when causing muscles to contract.

A person's capability to build strength partly depends on genetics. There are obvious factors, such as height and body type. In addition, tendon length and muscle fiber composition vary from one individual to another. Muscles consist of two

A magnified cross section of a single skeletal muscle fiber reveals that it is made up of smaller structures, which are called myosin filaments.

types of fibers: slow-twitch and fast-twitch. Fast-twitch muscles have a greater capability of increasing in size and strength. People born with a greater proportion of fast-twitch muscles may improve performance more quickly when starting a weight-training program.

# The Core

Some training programs specifically condition the "core" muscles. In general, the core is described as the muscles that control posture. Core training targets the abs in combination with the muscles that stabilize the hips and pelvis. A strong core can enhance athletic performance, protect against back injury, and improve balance.

# Working the Muscles

The most obvious benefit of weight training lies in increased muscle mass. Beginners who start a program with the goal of losing weight may be dismayed to find that they actually gain weight after they begin regular weight training. This is often due to increased lean body mass. Muscle is denser than fat, which means it has a greater weight. For men, 15 to 18 percent body fat is a healthy range. For women, it's 22 to 25 percent.

Most resistance training follows the model of progressive overload. An individual stresses the muscle by selecting a weight that is difficult to lift on the last rep of a set. This overload causes microscopic tears in the muscle fibers. The muscles rebuild and grow during the period between workouts. As strength increases, greater weights are required to reach overload. Therefore, weight is progressively increased, or the work-out is adapted to continue providing a challenge.

The final rep may cause soreness in a muscle, but it should not be acutely painful. Most experts advise against following the saying, "No pain, no gain." Experiencing pain during a workout could mean you have injured yourself. A stabbing pain followed by a lingering ache could mean you have strained or pulled a muscle. (Technically, a

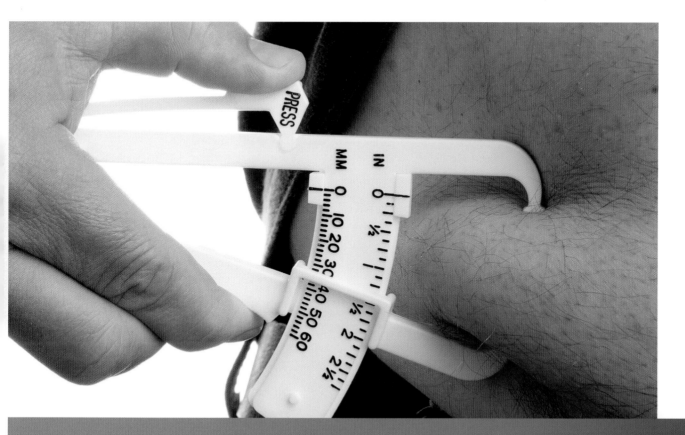

One way to determine body fat percentage is to check various parts of the body using calipers. Here, a man is having the body fat at his waist measured.

pull or strain actually affects the tendon.) Pain and swelling at a joint could indicate that you have a sprain. Sprains occur when you damage a ligament, the connective tissue between two bones. Poor form can cause carpal tunnel syndrome to develop in the wrists.

It is commonly believed that performing a low number of reps in a set is the best way to build strength and size, and that performing a high number builds muscular endurance. Some serious weight lifters test their strength by performing a one-rep max. This is the absolute limit of their strength, since they can only manage one rep. A one-rep max is too risky for most people, and it's not an effective way to build strength.

A computer image depicts muscles contracting as a man flexes his biceps. Skeletal muscles account for about 45 percent of body weight.

# About Your Muscles

There are about six hundred muscles in the human body. Many of them, such as the muscles of the face, hands, and spine, do not require exercise. Weight training targets major muscles and muscle groups in order to improve overall strength and fitness.

As a rule of thumb, it's a good idea to begin a workout by exercising the larger muscles before moving on to the smaller ones. The largest muscles in the upper body are in the chest and back, followed by the shoulders and arms, and then the wrists. In the lower body, the largest muscles are in the buttocks, followed by the thighs and lower legs. It's also essential to work the abdominal and lower-back muscles. When selecting weights for each exercise, remember that larger muscles are capable of lifting larger weights than smaller muscles are.

Chest exercises are extremely popular, especially with men who want to build an impressive physique. Strong chest muscles are also an asset in many sports and activities in which a strong upper body is needed. The muscles of the chest are called the pectorals, or pecs. The most notorious pec exercise is the bench press, in which you lie down on your back on a bench, lower a bar until it is nearly touching or just touching the chest, and then return it to the starting position. The amount a lifter can "bench" is often a point of pride, but overexerting yourself on the bench press can cause injury in the shoulders.

The upper-back muscles and the lower-back muscles are worked separately. The two major muscles in the upper back are the latissimus dorsi (or lats), the V-shaped muscles that meet in the center of the lower back, and the trapezius muscles (or traps), the diamond-shaped muscles that span the neck, shoulders, and back above the lats. The upper-back muscles benefit from exercises like chin-ups, rowing

Weights and weight machines are not always required for strength training. For exercises such as crunches, push-ups, and back extensions, your own body weight provides resistance.

exercises, and pull-downs, machine exercises in which you pull an overhead weight down to chest level. The key muscles of the lower back are the erector spinae muscles. There are various back-extension exercises that target these muscles.

The shoulder muscles consist of three muscles called the deltoids, or delts. Underneath the delts is the rotator cuff, a group of four muscles that prevent the arm bone from slipping out of the joint. Most shoulder exercises involve extending the arms above, in front of, or to the sides of the body. Improper form or straining to lift too much weight can easily injure the rotator cuffs.

There are two muscles in the upper arm: the biceps and triceps. The biceps, spanning the length in front of the arm bone, bend the arm. The triceps, to the back, straighten the arm. The best exercises for the biceps are curls, which generally involve bending the arms toward the body at the elbows. Most tricep exercises require that you straighten the arm against resistance. Exercises like wrist curls can strengthen the wrist.

The largest muscle in the body is the gluteus maximus, or glutes, the muscle that covers the entire buttocks. The hip flexors are located opposite the glutes in front of the hips. The major muscle on the sides of the hips is the gluteus medius, and the muscles on the inside of the thigh are called the abductors. The muscles in front of the thighs, which straighten the leg, are the quadriceps, or quads. The muscles behind the thigh, which bend the leg, are called hamstrings, or hams. The smaller muscles in the lower leg make up the calves and primarily work to move the feet.

An exercise known as the squat increases strength in the entire lower body. It requires you to stand with feet apart and squat as if sitting down in a chair, generally with a dumbbell in each hand or with a bar over the shoulders. Proper form and an appropriate amount of weight are essential for this exercise in order to avoid injury. In an exercise called the lunge, you take a long step forward with one foot and bend until the thigh is parallel to the floor. The opposite knee will bend down toward the floor. There are also various curls, presses, extensions, and lifts that target specific muscles in the lower body.

The abdominal muscles, or abs, are four muscles in the front of the torso. The standard exercise for strengthening the abs is the crunch. You lie down on the floor with knees bent, and you curl up so that the shoulders are raised. Then, you lower slowly. Be sure that you work your abs, not your neck, for this exercise. There are also numerous variations on the crunch, such as the reverse crunch, in which you raise the legs and use the abs to raise the hips slightly.

# Weight-Training Benefits

Many people weight train to improve their athletic performance. Others weight train to improve their physical appearance. Some weight train specifically for the health benefits to the muscles and bones. No matter what the motivation, weight training is a good practice for lifelong health.

Some people take it for granted that as people age, it's natural for them to lose strength, experience decreased bone density, and suffer from joint pain. After the age of twenty-five, muscle mass can decrease by a half pound each year. A weight-training program can stave off some of the effects of aging. Anybody, regardless of age, weight, or gender, can improve physical fitness and ensure better health for the future.

## Health and Lifestyle Benefits

Weight training benefits the entire musculoskeletal system. Just as it stresses muscles and makes them stronger, it also stresses bones and makes them stronger. Weight training helps maintain bone density

The lower back bears the most body weight and is the most likely site for back pain. Typical causes are poor posture, unfit muscles, obesity, and strain due to strenuous activity.

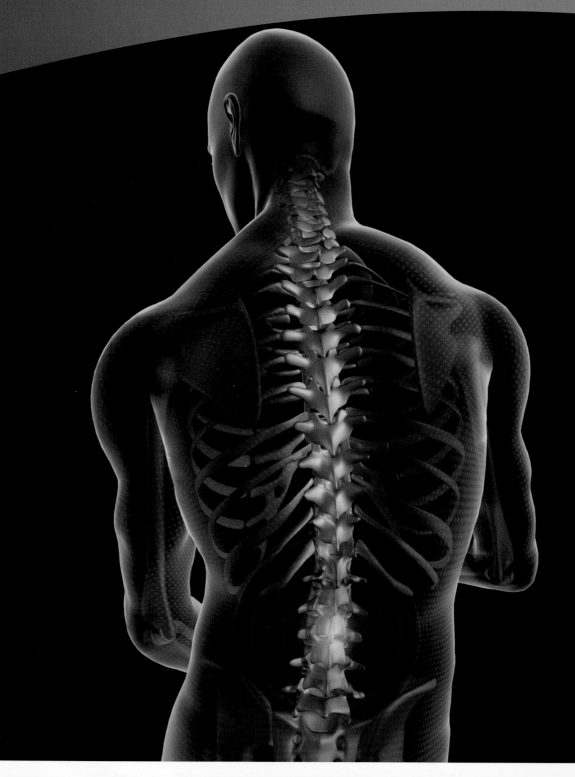

and slows down the loss of bone density that occurs with aging. Similarly, weight training strengthens the tendons and ligaments.

An increase in muscle mass leads to an increase in the body's metabolism, the rate at which calories are burnt. This is because when the body is at rest, muscles burn more calories than fat. For this reason, a weight-training program can help you maintain a healthy body weight for life. Weight training is also an essential part of a fitness program for people who are trying to lose weight. Weight training will not cause you to lose weight directly, but it will boost your abilities in sports and other physical activities, and it will help you maintain your weight loss.

Weight training helps reduce the risk of injury, sports-related or accidental. Toned muscles, joints, and ligaments are more resistant to damage. In addition, you are less likely to injure yourself doing strenuous activity. Some people, especially the elderly, have difficulty climbing stairs or lifting heavy shopping bags. Weight training can help prevent and even reverse loss of strength and reduce the resultant injuries.

One particularly important area with respect to injury prevention is the lower back. Many people experience back pain and injury, often as a consequence of many hours slouched at a desk. Sitting puts a great deal of pressure on the back. Strengthening the lower-back muscles can make it easier to maintain a proper posture while sitting.

In addition to the direct benefits, weight training improves overall health and well-being. People who weight train have better balance and flexibility. They sleep

# Gender Differences

There is no difference in muscle fiber between men and women. Both sexes have equivalent strength potential per pound of muscle. Men have a greater proportion of muscle in their upper bodies, while women have more muscle in their lower bodies. Overall, men have a larger size and greater muscle mass. Testosterone and other androgens, which are naturally occurring male sex hormones, promote muscle growth. Men have six to ten times the levels of androgens that women have.

better, have increased stamina, and reduce the risk of some diseases. Weight training can also ease the effects of some chronic conditions, such as arthritis or diabetes.

Lastly, weight training can give you confidence and improve your self-esteem. A weight-training program results in a fit, toned body and good posture. You will have the satisfaction of knowing that your dedication to your workout program paid off.

Most football players target every muscle group and aim to bulk up their muscles as much as possible, though specific strength requirements vary from one position to another.

# Conditioning for Athletic Performance

Strong muscles are essential for many sports and other physical activities. Whether you are a runner, climber, tennis player, diver, or wrestler, weight training can improve your performance. Many sports, such as soccer, football, and softball, require that players be able to move with speed and power. Weight training is a key element of the fitness program for these athletes—you will never see a top marathon runner with weak legs. Even for busy people who don't participate much in athletics, a weight-training program makes everyday tasks easier.

Many athletes give special attention to the muscles that are important in their sports. They address the specific demands of the sport and work to strengthen muscles that are prone to injury. Most weight-training guides give pointers on training for specific sports, and there are entire books dedicated to weight training for a specific sport.

Long-distance runners and some other endurance athletes have tended to be wary of weight training due to the belief that bulky muscles would slow them down. A weight-training program can promote balanced muscle development, however, and help prevent injury. Runners propel themselves forward with the hamstrings, and these muscles become strengthened as a result. This creates an imbalance in strength between the hamstrings and the quadriceps on the front of the legs. Therefore, runners are prone to back pain and other injuries that can be prevented by working the quadriceps. Runners should also work the muscles that affect posture, including the shoulders, back, and abs.

Cyclists often exhibit the problem opposite from that of runners. Cycling strengthens the quadriceps so that the hamstrings are relatively weak. Cyclists should work the hamstrings while strength training, as well as the upper-body muscles that control the bicycle.

Swimmers use different muscles for different strokes, so they require well-balanced strength for peak performance. Because the chest and shoulder muscles at the front of the body may be strengthened during swimming, athletes should work their upper back and shoulder muscles if a muscle imbalance develops.

Many sports are associated with certain injuries. Few people have heard of lateral epicondylitis, but they immediately recognize its nickname of "tennis elbow." Working the triceps and wrists can help prevent this type of injury. Similarly, golfers are prone to sore wrists and elbows. They should target the muscles of the

Swimmers use "dry land training" programs, which include cardio, weight, and flexibility conditioning, to improve their performance in the pool.

arms as well as the shoulders, lower back, hips, and legs. Exercising these muscles will add power to the swing and prevent back injury. Skiers can experience catastrophic injuries if they crash, and downhill skiers are prone to knee and back injuries. Skiers should work the quads and glutes, which control the skis, and the muscles of the upper body, which move the poles. These are only a few examples. Athletes in every sport can benefit from a weight-training program tailored to their needs.

# Weight-Training Concerns

## CHAPTER 4

As with any sport or other physical activity, weight training has its health and safety risks. Most of these risks involve careless, improper, or unwise use of the equipment. It's easy to make a clumsy mistake if your mind wanders. But when the mistake involves losing control of a heavy weight, it could have painful consequences. Errors like bad form, lifting weights too quickly, or failing to adjust a weight machine to your body size can result in injury. One key mistake is trying to show off by lifting too much weight—a sure route to an injury.

Attitude is important when undertaking a weight-training program. You should set realistic goals, such as improving your overall strength and athletic performance. Avoid setting goals like bulking up biceps and pecs without working any other muscles of the body or working out until you look like the cover model of a bodybuilding magazine. These types of goals are unhealthy and unrealistic. Also, remain eager to learn new exercises, techniques, and safety tips, even when you've mastered weight-training basics. There are always new ways that you can refine and improve your program.

## Know Your Limits

Before beginning a weight-training program, make sure you don't

A gym or athletic organization may be able to refer you to a doctor with experience in sports medicine, the field that specializes in injuries and other medical issues of athletes.

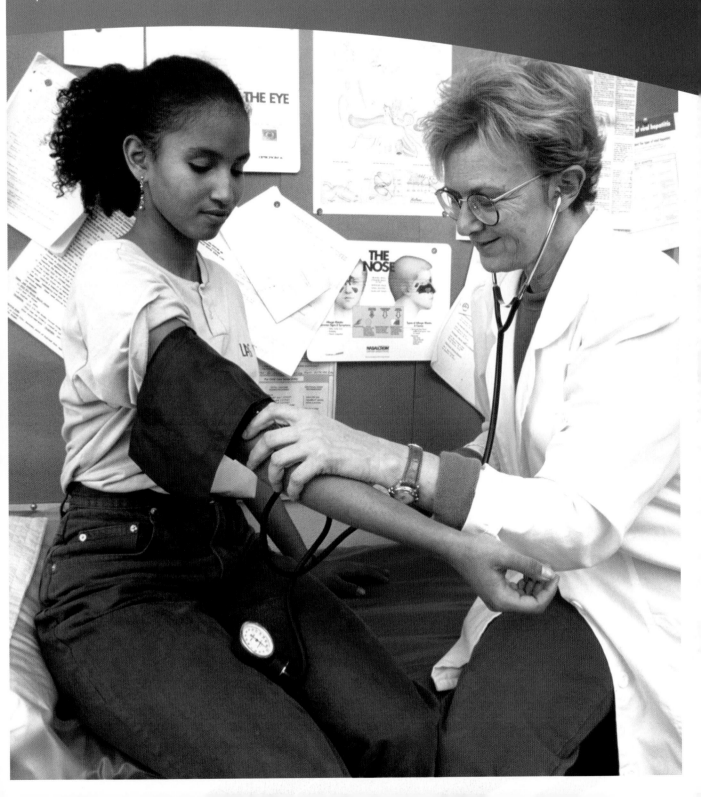

have any health problems that could affect your training. You should check with your doctor if you have symptoms that could indicate a medical condition. Start out by obtaining a copy of the Physical Activity Readiness Questionnaire (PAR-Q) and checking whether or not you have any of the health issues listed on the form. A medical condition does not exclude you from weight training, but it may require you to modify your program or become active more slowly. Examples of such conditions include obesity, diabetes, heart problems, asthma, high blood pressure, high cholesterol, or issues affecting the bones, muscles, ligaments, or tendons.

You may want to undergo a fitness appraisal. This is a collection of data like weight, blood pressure, heart rate, body composition, aerobic capacity, muscular strength, muscular endurance, and flexibility. A fitness appraisal offers a good starting point in planning a weight-training program. In addition, you will be able to track your progress over time and identify areas in which you can improve.

# The Myth of Spot Reducing

Many people target one specific part of their body when weight training. They might want to work on a slimmer waist or perhaps get rid of some of the flab on the upper arms. Such efforts will tone the muscles in the area, but it's not possible to "spot reduce" fat on one body part. The only way to lose fat is to reduce your overall body fat through diet and exercise.

## Weight-Training Safety

The potential for injury in the weight room begins the first time you pick up a weight from the rack. Many people who are otherwise careful grab and carry it with one hand, inviting injury before they even begin the workout. This method puts the body off-balance and can strain the back. The proper technique is to carry the weight close to the body using both hands.

Before beginning exercises, make sure you and your spotter both know the number of reps in the set and when you expect you might need help.

There are safety measures that apply to most weight-training exercises as well as precautions for specific exercises. In general, you should not hold your breath when lifting a weight. Holding your breath can affect your blood pressure, potentially causing dizziness or fainting. Lift weights smoothly and use proper form. Use an appropriate grip, or hand position, when lifting. Observe proper procedures and safety measures for machines—don't try to work your legs on a machine designed to exercise the arms, and use the safety belt if the machine has one.

Some of these precautions are commonsense measures, while others can be learned only through experience. If you have any doubt about the proper way to perform an exercise, or the right way to use a machine, ask a coach, teacher, or staff member.

For some free-weight exercises, you should have a spotter standing by. You don't need one for every exercise, but there are circumstances in which a spotter is necessary for your safety. You should ask someone to be your spotter if you're trying out a new exercise and may need help being guided through the unfamiliar movements. Get a spotter if you're increasing your weight for an exercise or if you're not sure that you'll be able to complete the last few reps of a set.

Spotting is an important responsibility. The spotter should be strong enough to provide adequate assistance. Communication is essential—the spotter must know what the lifter wants to accomplish and when the lifter may want assistance. Spotters may help position the weights. They may assist during the last couple of reps, or they may move in after an unsuccessful rep. A good spotter is attentive and offers encouragement, but he or she should not distract the lifter or provide assistance too soon. There are standard positions and techniques for spotters in many exercises. During the bench press, for example, the spotter stands behind the bench with his or her hands close to the bar.

# Be Realistic

Weight training is great for health and performance, but it cannot give everyone a sculpted physique bulging with muscles. People respond to weight training differently depending on their body type and genetics. You should strive to achieve your personal optimal performance, rather than try to outdo your friends or compare yourself to professional athletes.

Nonetheless, some people develop unhealthy habits in an attempt to build strength and muscle mass, or acquire a lean, toned body. People who spend too

Anabolic steroids are synthetic hormones that act to increase muscle size and power. High doses are required for significant gains, increasing side effects and long-term health risks.

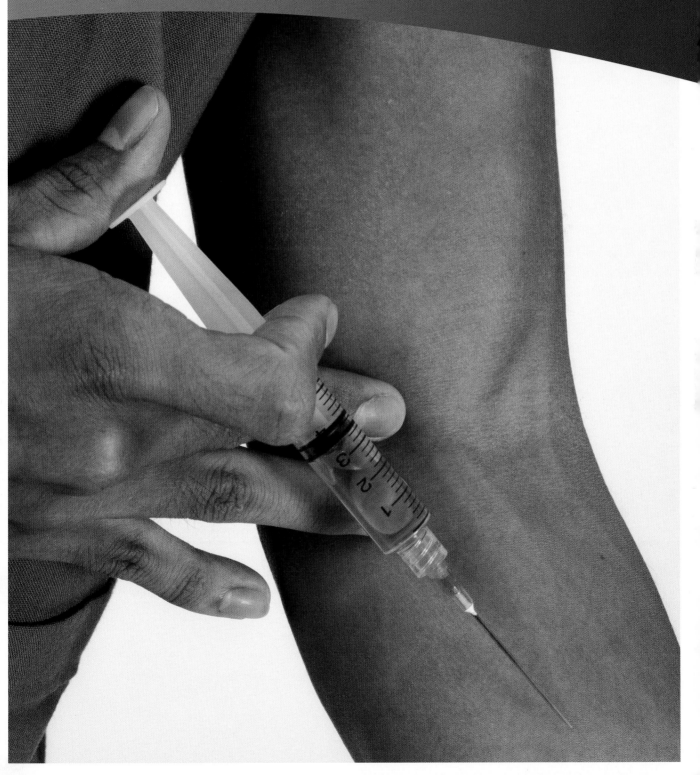

much time training are in danger of overtraining. The body can handle only a certain intensity of weight training. Performance declines when a person has been overtraining, and he or she may experience fatigue, extreme soreness, disturbed sleep, and depression. If someone has been overtraining, the best remedy is to take a few days off and reduce the intensity of the program in the future.

Some people obsessed with building muscle mass resort to anabolic steroids, a risky and illegal way of enhancing performance. Anabolic steroids are drugs that promote muscle growth. Steroids have dangerous side effects, particularly among adolescents who can have their normal growth disrupted by using the drugs. Steroids also leave users vulnerable to injury, since muscle growth isn't accompanied by any increase of strength in tendons and ligaments.

People obsessed with reducing their weight and body fat may develop eating disorders like anorexia or bulimia. Anorexics drastically restrict the amount of food they eat, sometimes allowing their weight to fall dangerously low. Bulimics swing between dieting and binging, in which they consume a huge amount of food in a short amount of time and usually force themselves to vomit afterwards. Most anorexics and bulimics are women, but men are not immune from eating disorders. Wrestlers and jockeys, for example, are at a higher-than-average risk of developing eating disorders because of weight restrictions in their sports.

# Beyond the Basics

To get the greatest benefit from weight training, your program should be one component of an overall healthy lifestyle. Your fitness program should also include flexibility and cardiovascular exercises. Make nutritious choices in your diet, get plenty of rest, and handle stress in a healthy manner.

Once you've mastered basic weight training, you may wonder what steps to take next. One good way to track your progress is to keep a training log. From day to day, you should record which exercises you perform, along with the weight, number of sets, and number of reps. If you find that there is a muscle group in which you have not met your goals, consider modifying your routine for that muscle group. Keeping a training log will also help you maintain a varied and balanced routine.

If you want to expand your weight-training experiences, you can enroll in a weight-training class, work with a personal trainer, join a health club, or learn some advanced lifting techniques. Even if you don't have the time or money for these options, you can learn a lot from books, fitness magazines, videos, and online resources.

## The Next Step

For many people, the best way to make weight-training progress is

Keeping a training log can be a great source of motivation. You will be able to monitor your improved performance and refine your routine to achieve greater benefits.

to join a gym or health club. There are many equipment options available at a gym or health club, and staff members are present to give you training tips. The facility will probably have a pool, cardio machines like exercise bikes, and other amenities.

If you join a gym, your fellow gym members will appreciate it if you behave with courtesy and attention to safety. Be aware of the people around you when you're carrying weights that could cause injury when dropped. Return your weights to the rack, and place a towel on the bench or other piece of equipment before beginning your exercise.

A personal trainer can design a program and offer tips specific to your needs. Look for a trainer certified by an organization such as the American College of Sports Medicine.

One of the most effective—yet expensive—ways to improve your routine is to work with a personal trainer. A personal trainer can guide a novice lifter from the initial fitness assessment to the achievement of his or her fitness goals. Along the way, the trainer explains the equipment, safety precautions, proper form, and techniques. A personal trainer is well qualified to recommend exercises that are best suited to the lifter's needs and goals or evaluate when a weight-training program should be modified.

An alternative is to enroll in a group weight-training class. In most cases, your classmates will be other people with your level of ability. There are beginner classes,

Weight training provides women with immediate results, such as a well-toned body, as well as long-term benefits, such as improved bone density, which can reduce the risk of osteoporosis.

classes intended for teens, and classes geared toward working just the lower body or other specific area. The class may use free weights, elastic bands, and other equipment, or you may participate in group circuit training. Members of a circuit class work their way through a series of weight-training machines, usually spending a timed period on each machine.

## Cutting-Edge Weight Training

Experts used to advise endurance athletes to minimize their weight training, fearing it could add bulky muscle. Today, it's recognized that almost all athletes benefit from weight training. Most new discoveries about it confirm that it can help practically everyone improve their health, even the elderly, pregnant women, and those who are inactive. Today, many women have embraced weight training, recognizing that it will not add unwanted bulk to their frames. Children can even benefit from weight training and form good fitness habits from a young age. They must be careful not to overstrain themselves, however, since their bodies are still developing.

It's sometimes difficult to separate fads from genuine breakthroughs in weight training. During the late 1990s, for example, there was a period of national obsession with toned abs. Companies developed a number of devices for working abs. Most fitness professionals, however, believed that the same or better results could be accomplished with crunches and other floor exercises.

There are a number of weight-training variations that you can add to your routine. You can try "superset," in which you perform two different exercises

## The Stretching Debate

You might be surprised to hear that there is controversy surrounding healthy stretching. Most experts agree that regular stretching is important in limbering up the muscles, maintaining flexibility, and loosening the joints. There is disagreement, however, on the best stretching technique and on whether or not stretching even prevents injury. Some studies show that traditional stretching can actually cause injury. Many trainers now recommend that you stretch after a workout, not before.

consecutively with no break in between. The SuperSlow method calls for you to spend about fifteen seconds per rep. Negatives are lifts in which you only lower the weight—the "negative" phase. (The lifting phase is the concentric phase.) Some cutting-edge techniques are controversial. Functional strength training focuses on muscle movement to a greater degree than traditional strength training, which emphasizes muscle strength. The movements should resemble movements that people make in their athletic activities or daily lives. With common sense, expertise, and a bit of research, you should be able to determine which exercises are just fads and which are genuine innovations in building strength.

# GLOSSARY

**calorie**  A unit of heat that is used to measure the energy-producing potential in food.

**cardiovascular**  Pertaining to the heart, lungs, and circulatory system.

**carpal tunnel syndrome**  A medical condition of the hand and wrist caused by compression of a nerve in the wrist.

**fiber**  An elongated, threadlike cell in the body.

**joint**  The point of connection of two bones.

**ligament**  The connective tissue between bones.

**metabolism**  The chemical processes in the body that are necessary to maintain life.

**osteoporosis**  A disease, most common in older women, in which the bones become porous and fragile.

**overload**  An amount of weight that causes stress in the body.

**overtraining**  A condition characterized by fatigue and decreased performance, caused by too little recovery time after training.

**repetition**  One execution of an exercise; also called a rep.

**resistance**  A mechanical force that tends to retard or oppose motion; in weight training, the body works against resistance.

**set**  A series of reps performed without stopping for rest.

**spotter**  Someone who assists a lifter during an exercise.

**stamina**  Physical ability to withstand fatigue.

**tendon**  The tissue that connects muscle to bone.

# FOR MORE INFORMATION

American College of Sports Medicine (ACSM)
401 West Michigan Street
Indianapolis, IN 46202-3233
(317) 637-9200
Web site: http://www.acsm.org
The ACSM is the largest sports medicine and exercise science organization in
the world.

American Council on Exercise (ACE)
4851 Paramount Drive
San Diego, CA 92123
(858) 279-8227
Web site: http://www.acefitness.org
The ACE is an organization committed to enriching quality of life through safe
and effective exercise and physical activity.

Canadian Association for the Advancement of Women and Sport and
Physical Activity
N202-801 King Edward Avenue
Ottawa, ON K1N 6N5
Canada
(613) 562-5667
Web site: http://www.caaws.ca
This group advocates equal opportunities for women in sports.

National Strength and Conditioning Association (NSCA)
1885 Bob Johnson Drive
Colorado Springs, CO 80906
(719) 632-6722
Web site: http://www.nsca-lift.org
The NSCA is a leading authority on strength and conditioning.

Physical and Health Education Canada (PHE)
301-2197 Riverside Drive
Ottawa, ON K1H 7X3
Canada
(613) 523-1348
Web site: http://www.cahperd.ca
The PHE is an organization that advocates and educates for quality physical and
    health education programs.

Presidential Council on Physical Fitness and Sports
Department W
200 Independence Avenue SW, Room 738-H
Washington, DC 20201-0004
(202) 690-9000
Web site: http://www.fitness.gov
This government organization provides information on health, physical activity,
    fitness, and sports.

## Web Sites

Due to the changing nature of Internet links, Rosen Publishing has developed an
online list of Web sites related to the subject of this book. This site is updated regu-
larly. Please use this link to access the list:

http://www.rosenlinks.com/hwe/weight

# FOR FURTHER READING

Bellenir, Karen, ed. *Fitness Information for Teens*. Detroit, MI: Omnigraphics, 2004.

Burke, Edmund R., Ph.D. *Optimal Muscle Performance and Recovery*. 2nd ed. New York, NY: Avery, 2003.

Delavier, Frederic. *Strength Training Anatomy: Your Illustrated Guide to Muscles at Work*. 2nd ed. Champaign, IL: Human Kinetics, 2006.

The Diagram Group. *The Facts On File Illustrated Guide to the Human Body*. New York, NY: Facts On File, 2005.

Fahey, Thomas. *Weight Training Basics: A Complete Program for Men and Women*. New York, NY: McGraw Hill, 2005.

Kraemer, William J., and Steven J. Fleck. *Strength Training for Young Athletes*. 2nd ed. Champaign, IL: Human Kinetics, 2004.

Raskin, Donna. *The Everything Fitness Book: Lose Weight, Build Strength, and Feel Energized*. 2nd ed. Avon, MA: Adams Media, 2007.

Sandler, David. *Weight Training Fundamentals: A Better Way to Learn the Basics*. Champaign, IL: Human Kinetics, 2003.

# BIBLIOGRAPHY

Archer, Shirley S. *The Everything Weight Training Book: Tone, Shape, and Strengthen Your Body—Look Your Best in No Time*. Avon, MA: Adams Media, 2002.

Fahey, Thomas. *Basic Weight Training for Men and Women*. 6th ed. New York, NY: McGraw Hill, 2006.

Johnson-Cane, Deirdre, Jonathan Cane, and Joe Glickman. *The Complete Idiot's Guide to Weight Training*. 2nd ed. Indianapolis, IN: Alpha Books, 2003.

MayoClinic.com. "Strength Training: Get Stronger, Leaner, and Healthier." Mayo Foundation for Medical Education and Research, July 4, 2008. Retrieved December 12, 2008 (http://www.mayoclinic.com/health/strength-training/HQ01710).

Neporent, Liz, and Suzanne Schlosberg. *Weight Training for Dummies*. 3rd ed. Hoboken, NJ: Wiley Publishing, 2006.

Vella, Mark. *Anatomy for Strength and Fitness Training: An Illustrated Guide to Your Muscles in Action*. New York, NY: McGraw Hill, 2006.

# INDEX

## About the Author

Corona Brezina has written more than a dozen titles for Rosen Publishing. Several of her previous books have also focused on topics related to health issues facing young adults, including *Uppers: Stimulant Abuse* from the Incredibly Disgusting Drugs series. She lives in Chicago.

## Photo Credits

Cover and interior (silhouetted figures) © www.istockphoto.com/Simon Spoon; cover and interior (stripe graphics) © www.istockphoto.com/Brandon Laufenberg; cover and p. 1 (circulatory system figure), p. 22 © www.istockphoto.com/Mads Abildgaard; pp. 5, 7, 8, 12, 19, 26, 33, 36, 38 Shutterstock.com; p. 10 © www.istockphoto.com/diego_cervo; p. 15 © Visuals Unlimited/Corbis; p. 17 © www.istockphoto.com/Jim DeLillo; p. 18 © Friedrich Saurer/Photo Researchers, Inc.; p. 24 © www.istockphoto.com/Bill Grove; p. 29 © Michael Newman/PhotoEdit; p. 31 © www.istockphoto.com/Tomaz Levstek; p. 37 © www.istockphoto.com/Rich Legg.

Designer: Nicole Russo; Editor: Nicholas Croce;
Photo Researcher: Cindy Reiman